DESIGN IT!

INTERIOR DESIGN

Alix Wood

Gareth Stevens
PUBLISHING

Please visit our website, **www.garethstevens.com**.
For a free color catalog of all our high-quality books,
call toll free 1-800-542-2595 or fax 1-877-542-2596

Cataloging-in-Publication Data
Names: Wood, Alix.
Title: Interior design / Alix Wood.
Description: New York : Gareth Stevens Publishing, 2018. | Series: Design it! | Includes index.
Identifiers: ISBN 9781538207987 (pbk.) | ISBN 9781538207963 (library bound) |
    ISBN 9781538207840 (6 pack)
Subjects: LCSH: House furnishings--Juvenile literature. | Decoration and ornament--Juvenile
    literature. | Handicraft--Juvenile literature. | Interior decoration--Juvenile literature.
Classification: LCC TX315.W66 2018 | DDC 747.7'7--dc23

First Edition

Published in 2018 by
Gareth Stevens Publishing
111 East 14th Street, Suite 349
New York, NY 10003

Produced for Gareth Stevens by Alix Wood Books
Designed by Alix Wood
Editor: Eloise Macgregor
Editor for Gareth Stevens: Kerri O'Donnell

Photo credits: Cover, 1, 3, 8, 9, 10, 11, 12, 13, 14, 15, 16, 17, 18, 19, 20, 21, 22, 23, 24, 25, 26, 27, 28, 29
© Alix Wood; 4, 5, 6, 7 © Adobe Stock Images

Printed in the United States of America
CPSIA compliance information: Batch # CS17GS: For further information contact Gareth Stevens, New York, New York at 1-800-542-2595.

CONTENTS

GET DESIGNING

Would you like to make your home or classroom look amazing? **Interior designers** plan how the rooms of a building should be furnished and decorated. The word "interior" just means the inside of a place.

It's a **creative** and artistic job. It's fun to make your room look just the way you want it. There are so many different things you can do. Try the projects in this book and make your space your own.

CHOOSING A COLOR SCHEME

One of the most important decisions to make is to decide on a **color scheme**. Designers use a color wheel like this one to help pick out colors. Which are your favorites?

Design Tips

Colors that are opposite each other on a color wheel are called **complementary colors**. They look really bold and striking when used together.

There are many different ways to combine colors. You can use all **shades** of the same color. This style is called **monochromatic**. The word comes from the Greek language, where "mono" means "one," and "khroma" means "color."

pink and green are complementary colors

designers often use colors that are next to each other on the color wheel

When you are at home you probably spend the most time in your bedroom. It's great if you can design your room so it reflects your personality. Designers often choose a theme for a room. You could choose anything you want. How about a jungle theme or a castle theme?

When you choose a theme for your room, make sure it isn't something that you will grow out of quickly.

SAMPLE BOARDS

How will you know if your design choices will look good together? Designers create a **sample** board. A sample board is a **collage** made up of fabrics, colors, and images of furniture and **accessories**. It really helps get an idea of how your design will look.

Designers use their sample board to show **clients** their ideas. Make one yourself to show your parents or caregivers. They might let you try some of your designs.

Design Tips

Keep a design scrap box. You can usually take samples of wallpaper from DIY stores to put in your box. Whenever you see something that you can't take, take a photo of it, instead. You can make a folder on your computer to put things that **inspire** you, too.

MAKE A SAMPLE BOARD

Sample boards help you see whether your ideas look good together. Using scraps and free samples means a board won't cost any money to make, so you can afford to make a few mistakes along the way.

1 Collect scraps and pictures of anything that has caught your eye. Try to keep a color scheme in mind as you select items. Arrange your selections on the board.

2 Discard anything that doesn't work in your scheme. Keep adding to your board until you are happy with the "look." Now you are ready to present your ideas.

ROOM PLANNING

Designers usually make a plan of each room before they start work. Drawing a plan lets them try different furniture **layouts** really easily. It beats moving all the furniture around!

To make a plan, first measure your room. Draw your plan on some squared paper. You will need to decide on a **scale**. That is, how many squares will equal a foot or a meter. On this drawing one large square = 1 foot (0.3 m).

Measure your furniture. Using the same scale, cut out a paper shape for each piece of furniture and label it. Now you can move the shapes around to find the best layout for your room.

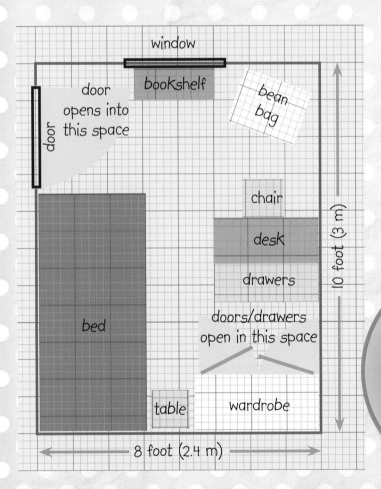

window
bookshelf
door opens into this space
door
bean bag
chair
desk
drawers
doors/drawers open in this space
bed
table
wardrobe
10 foot (3 m)
8 foot (2.4 m)

Design Tips

Think about how you need to use your room. Is there enough space to walk around and to open any drawers or doors? The gray quarter-circles in this plan show the space a door needs to swing open.

If you share a room, can you give each of you some private space?

MAKE A SHOE BOX ROOM PLAN

Flat plans are great for figuring out where your furniture should go. How can you see if all your colors will work together? The best way is to make a model of your room. Designers usually do this using computer software, but you can make a model using a shoe box.

YOU WILL NEED:
- a shoe box
- scraps of material
- card stock or wallpaper samples
- glue
- scissors

1 Choose your colors. Cut the card stock or wallpaper to fit by tracing around the side of the box and then cutting just inside the line you have drawn. Glue in place.

2

Make furniture out of card stock. You can just tape folded strips of card stock to make any legs.

3 You can create card dots using a hole punch. Cut strips of card stock to make stripes. Glue them in place. Use scrap fabric to make bedding. If you don't like anything, it's easy to change it.

THUMBTACK ART

You can make some great art for your room using simple thumbtacks. You can use colored thumbtacks to make patterns, or pictures. Remember, thumbtacks can be dangerous, particularly for young children, so make sure you hang your art out of reach.

1

Place your black card stock on top of your cardboard and draw around the card stock. Test the depth by pushing in a thumbtack. You want it to be thick enough so that the pin doesn't stick out the back.

2

Trace around another sheet of cardboard if one sheet isn't deep enough. Then cut the sheets just inside the outline you drew. If you needed more than one sheet, glue the sheets together.

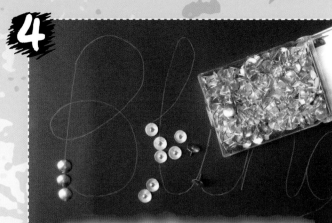

3

Using the white pencil, write something onto the black card stock. It could be a name or a phrase. The writing will need to be big so it is easy to create using the thumbtacks.

4

Push the thumbtacks along the lines of your writing. Line up the tacks so they just touch once they are pushed all the way in.

5

To hang your picture, push two more thumbtacks into the cardboard at the back and tie some thread or string to them. Use the thread to hang your picture on a nail on your wall.

FUN LIGHTING

The right lighting is important. Think about what your room will be used for. A work area might need bright light but a relaxation area might require a softer glow. One really cheap and easy way to decorate your room is to color some lightbulbs. Light up your room with these fun lightbulb designs.

1

Ask an adult to select a suitable lightbulb for you to decorate. You need to be sure the bulb is the right type for your light fitting. Use markers with good strong colors.

2

For this rainbow lightbulb, divide the lightbulb into equal stripes by drawing a small mark in each color along the bulb. Then start coloring in the sections.

3

Continue to add your stripes as you go down the lightbulb. A rainbow goes red, orange, yellow, green, blue, indigo, violet. Be careful where the colors meet that they don't smudge each other.

4

The finished lightbulb should look something like this. Make sure your coloring is solid. Any gaps will let too much plain light through and spoil the effect.

Different colors and designs will make different patterns on the walls. Try drawing some patterns or pictures in a colored marker that matches your room's color scheme.

NINJA BOX

Make a ninja warrior container to guard your stuff. These tall containers are so easy to make, you could make a Ninja army! They are great for keeping things like rulers and paintbrushes in.

1

Mark a line all around the carton, a little way from the top. Cut along the line using scissors. You may need an adult to help you.

2

Wrap the black card stock around the carton, leaving a small overlap at one edge. One A4 sheet will usually cover a juice carton. Trim away any card that overlaps the top or bottom.

3

Draw a rectangle near the top of one side, using the white pencil. Push the scissors into the center of the rectangle, and carefully cut around the outline.

4

Tape some white card behind the rectangle hole. Decorate your ninja's face. We used wobbly eyes bought from a craft store, but you can use marker. Color the face using crayon.

5

Wrap red tape on the end of the ninja's stick to make a handle. Fold a strip of blue electrical tape lengthwise to make a belt for your ninja.

6

Glue the card stock to the carton. Neaten the top edge by folding over strips of black electrical tape.

Design Tips

This project would look fantastic in a room with Asian decor. You could mix in a Japanese screen or some bamboo matting (below).

FANCY FLOWERPOTS

It's good to have plants in your room. They look good and they are even good for you as they produce fresh **oxygen**. Make them **coordinate** with your decor by personalizing their plant pots.

1

To make a **template**, mark some masking tape and place it on the pot's rim. Lay your flowerpot on the paper with the mark facing down. Roll the pot, drawing a line at the top and bottom, until it has rolled full circle and the mark is facing down.

YOU WILL NEED:
- fabric
- an old paintbrush
- flowerpot
- school glue
- newspaper
- string
- masking tape
- a marker
- some paper

2

Cut out the template. Lay it on your fabric and draw a line around it a little bit larger than the template, so you have enough fabric to overlap the bottom of the pot.

Design Tips

Because a flowerpot curves, stripes will slant at some points. If this bothers you, choose a different patterned fabric.

3

Put down some newspaper. Using an old paintbrush, spread glue all over the flowerpot. Carefully press the fabric around the pot. Fold over the fabric at the bottom, as shown.

4

Spread glue around the rim. Turning the pot, wind some string several times around the rim.

PAINTED FLOWERPOT

You can paint flowerpots, using tempera paint. Wait for each color to completely dry before you paint over it. Seal the flowerpot inside and out with school glue. Otherwise the damp soil may spoil the paint or fabric.

BRAID A RAG RUG

Try making your own braided rug for your room. Collect plenty of scrap fabric. You can make a small rug out of around six adult T-shirts. Rugs usually look best if you stick to two or three main colors

1

Measure and then cut your fabric into long strips, between 1 and 2 inches (2.5 and 5 cm) wide. Use a white pencil to mark the fabric before you cut.

2

Tie three strips of fabric together. Start to braid the strips. Long strips may get tangled as you braid, so take care to untangle them as you go.

Design Tips

If you use old T-shirts, try to cut your strips in a long spiral from the bottom hem then up and around the body.

3

To add new strips, simply tie them to the end of a strip as it runs out. Try to keep all the knots on one side of the rug as you braid.

4

You need a long braid to make a decent-sized rug. Measure it as you go, to check you have made enough.

Ask an adult to help sew the rug together. Wrap the braid into a spiral. Sew from the center out, joining the braid to the increasing spiral.

LEAF BOWL

Did you know you can make a bowl out of leaves! This is a fun project to do in the fall. Go outside and collect the most colorful leaves you can find. If you can't find any or it's the wrong time of year, you can use craft store fabric leaves.

Design Tips

This bowl needs patience. It is important to make sure the glue dries completely before you pop the balloon.

YOU WILL NEED:
- some different colored leaves
- school glue
- an old paintbrush
- a flowerpot
- a balloon
- some string

1

Blow up the balloon, and tie a length of string to the end. Using an old paintbrush, completely cover the other round end with school glue.

2

Thread the string through the hole in the bottom of the flowerpot. Pull the string until the balloon sits snugly in the pot. This should hold your balloon still while you glue the leaves.

3

Start to stick your leaves on to the balloon. Once the balloon looks how you want it to, paint over it with the school glue. Don't worry if the glue looks white at this point, it will be see-through once it dries.

4

Cover the leaves with another layer of glue. Let the glue dry and then apply another layer. After 2 days, pop the balloon.

CHILL-OUT ZONE

If you share a bedroom, you might want to create a private space where you can get away from it all. Try making this simple tepee den.

YOU WILL NEED:
- garden stakes
- some string
- a throw or a blanket
- a rug or some cushions

1

Take three tall garden stakes. Arrange them into a tepee shape, and then tie them together at the top. Next, tie on two more stakes and arrange them.

2

To make your tepee nice and sturdy, add five small supporting stakes. Tie them tightly to the bottom of the tall stakes to create a hexagon.

3

Find a large, colorful throw or blanket. Wrap it around the structure. You may need someone to help you hold it while you tie it tightly to the top of the tepee.

4

Now it is time to get comfortable. Find a fluffy rug or some cushions. Grab some books, shut the flap, and snuggle down.

FUNKY FEET

You could decorate a little chair to go in your tepee. Choose some colorful socks and stuff the toes with newspaper. Put them on your chair's legs!

MOSAIC FRAME

Make a custom picture frame for your room out of cardboard and magazine cuttings. Choose colors that look good with both the picture and the room.

YOU WILL NEED:
- two cardboard squares
- a glue stick
- old magazines
- tempera paint
- scissors

1

Measure the photograph that you want to frame. Make the central hole in a cardboard square just a little smaller than the picture.

2

To cut out the central square, pierce the middle with scissors and then cut to each corner of your square. It's then easier to cut along the lines.

3

You should end up with two cardboard squares, one with a square hole in the middle.

4

Choose the colors that you want your **mosaic** frame to be. Cut out squares of your colors. Glossy, shiny magazine pages work best.

5

Paint the cardboard that will go at the back of your frame a nice, contrasting color. Paint the frame itself using white tempera paint. You may need to use two coats.

6

Wait for the paint to dry. Then, using the glue stick, stick the mosaic squares on to the front of your frame. Glue the frame together, leaving one side open so you can slide in your photograph.

PENNANTS

Do you want your room to have a party feel all year round? Try making these colorful pennants. It's really easy to make this version out of card stock. They don't need any sewing at all.

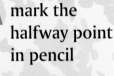

mark the halfway point in pencil

1

halve each half and mark that too

2

You can get three triangles out of a sheet of card. Mark the points as shown above. Using a ruler and pencil join the points together in a "W" shape. Cut along the lines.

Get a sheet of contrasting card stock. To make the spot design, draw around a small spool of thread or a penny. Repeat this several times.

3

Carefully cut out your circles. Rub each circle over the glue stick, and press them on to some of the triangles. Keep your fingers away from the glue or you may mess up your card.

4

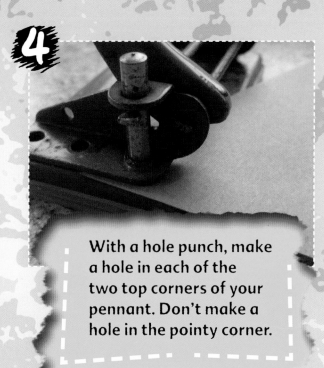

With a hole punch, make a hole in each of the two top corners of your pennant. Don't make a hole in the pointy corner.

Design Tips

If you want to make a pennant to hang outside, you could use colorful thick plastic bags instead of card stock.

5

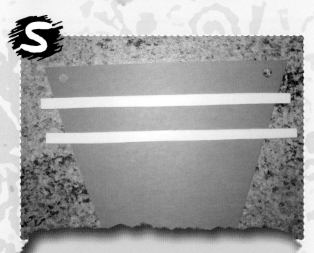

Cut your contrasting card stock into strips. Stick them on some of the pennants. Don't worry if the strips overlap the edge, you can trim them off with scissors.

6

Thread the string through the holes at the top of your triangles. Now you can hang your pennant in your room.

MAKE ART

Haven't got anything to go on the walls that matches your color scheme? No problem. Create your own simple art.

1

Using masking tape, divide your canvas up into interesting shapes. If you are using a thick canvas, extend the tape around the sides, too.

2

Mix up several shades of paint that will go well with your room's color scheme.

Design Tips

Five or six different shades will usually be enough. You want to try to paint areas that are next to each other in a different shade.

3

Apply the paint using a sponge. Dab, don't drag, or else some of the paint might go under the tape.

4

If you are using a thick canvas like this one, remember to take your color around the sides too.

5

Wait until your paint is completely dry. It is best to leave it overnight. Then, gently pull off the masking tape to reveal the white lines.

GLOSSARY

accessories Objects that are not necessary, but that add to the beauty of a room.

clients People who use the professional advice or services of another.

collage A work of art made by gluing pieces of different materials to a flat surface.

color scheme An arrangement or combination of colors.

complementary colors Colors that when placed next to each other create the strongest contrast.

coordinate To go together smoothly.

creative Showing imagination.

inspire To stimulate to greater or higher activity.

interior designers People who design the interiors of rooms or buildings.

layouts The ways in which a room can be arranged.

monochromatic Using only one color.

mosaic A picture or pattern produced by arranging small pieces of stone, tile, glass, etc.

oxygen A colorless, tasteless, odorless gas that is necessary for life.

sample A small part or quantity intended to show what the whole is like.

scale Size in comparison.

shade The darkness or lightness of a color.

template Something that establishes or serves as a pattern.

FOR MORE INFORMATION

Books

Allen, Katherine. *Emily's Room: Creating Spaces that Unlock Your Potential*. Boise, ID: Tru Publishing, 2015.

Kraft, Ellen Christiansen. *Doodle Design & Draw DREAM ROOMS*. Mineola, NY: Dover Doodle Books, 2012.

Smith, Tana. *DIY Bedroom Decor: 50 Awesome Ideas for Your Room*. Avon, MA: Adams Media, 2015.

Websites

Kids Think Design website. Meet a designer and take part in a design project to make your classroom look better
http://www.kidsthinkdesign.org/interiors/index.html

INDEX